WAVE
OF THE DAY
Collected Poems

WAVE OF THE DAY

Collected Poems

MARY ELIZABETH WINN

Rootstock Publishing

First Printing: February 2017

WAVE OF THE DAY
Copyright © 2017 by Mary Elizabeth Winn

ISBN-10: 1-57869-001-3
ISBN-13: 978-1-57869-001-5
Library of Congress Control Number: 2017901005
Multicultural Media, Montpelier, VERMONT

Published by Rootstock Publishing
An Imprint of Multicultural Media Inc.
27 Main Street, Suite 6
Montpelier, VT 05602 USA
info@multiculturalmedia.com

This book is a work of fiction. Names, characters,
places, and incidents either are products of the author's
imagination or are used fictitiously. Any resemblance
to actual persons, living or dead, events, or locales is
entirely coincidental.

Email the family: *diana@reboprecords.com*

Cover and book design by Carrie Cook

Printed in the USA.

*Dedicated to Oliver Winn,
Mary's husband of 70 years, and to "the children
of our loving," Michael, Diana, Charles, and
Elizabeth, as well as for those who, much to her
surprise, appeared beside her in widowhood,
to love and be loved.*

TABLE OF CONTENTS

PROLOGUE

Mary Elizabeth Winn was 94 when planning began for publication of her collection of poems, written over her lifetime. Each, as she says, "holds something to think about."

She kept her poems in journals and in a handful of loose dog-eared paper. Through the ritual of transcribing her beautiful cursive pieces to digital docs, organizing her poems into new waves of meaning, her love and her story has unfolded in a totally unforeseen way. Even at 94, she continued to provide her family and friends with a strong, inexhaustible love.

Mary Elizabeth Winn was most proud and fulfilled to be a Mother and Teacher of children, four to be exact. She said it was what she knew she most wanted, since the age of three—to be blessed with a home, a strong marriage, and children to love.

Mary Elizabeth was always a Maker—a maker of art, of poems, of clothing for herself, her children and grandchildren, as well as for the meticulously and beautifully dressed dolls in her extensive collection. She became a devoted and exceptionally talented Home Maker, making one house after another a beautiful home for the Winn family over the years—in upstate New York, Schenectady, Skaneateles, Whitesboro, Glens Falls, Cazenovia, and then later, in Marlton, New Jersey, and Corona del Mar, California—and in the one enduring place that continues to feel most like home to her children and grandchildren, the beloved cottage on Lake George.

Mary was always a Learner, a self-made scholar, a ravenous reader, an observer, a philosopher, a reflective documenter through words and drawings, a perennial well-rounded student. She was an out of the ordinary kind of learner.

She took World War II-era flying lessons at the age of 20, one of only two women allowed in a class of 10. At the age of 83, she finished the college degree that had been cut short by her 1942 train ride to Schenectady to begin her life with Oliver. The final project of her Skidmore College Fine Arts degree—a book titled, *Pictures of the Pinelands,* expresses a young girl's experience of the Pine Barrens of New Jersey in joyful childlike poems and beautiful watercolors.

She was a curious, exploring kind of Learner, as in her adventures traveling with her husband over the years, ranging from the Georgian Islands to Puerto Rico, from Singapore to England. She wrote her personal observations and insights all along the way.

The unanticipated magic that has occurred in the process of recording Mary's rich retrospective of her bountiful life gives the reader words for what the human heart struggles to handle and express.

The epilogue on page 67, by one of Mary's daughters, is written especially for hospice workers, caregivers and families losing loved ones.

I

CHILDHOOD

BEFORE MY BIRTHING

I sat upon a rainbow
enfolded by a sea of colors
various beyond my knowing
their shades and tints undulating
unformed
beckoning.

> Chosen
> from among all the waiting others
> I grasped the rainbow
> all my hands could hold
> of what colors would be mine
> their shades and tints
> undulating
> malleable
> Mine.
> > I left behind
> > more of the rainbow sea.
> > It was for the waiting others
> > not for me.

It was for the waiting others
to grasp in their turn
and know
the brilliance
and the depth
of the colors that they hold.

I watch
I learn
I feed upon
all the love that I can gather,
I catch at colors and I weave.
A patterned fabric forms
and that's the way it is.
    The days
    overtake the days
    and not so many dance ahead
    with their pretty colors beckoning
    to wave at me.
    I hold the fabric in my hands,
    with unfinished pattern and
            the mystery
    of how to use the ribbons that I have
    to fill it out,
    to cover me.

The Shores, Shelburne

LULLABY

Sleep, my love, and know a resting.
Clear your brow of hurting things.
Drift upon Love's river lightly.
Know a joy that dreaming brings.

Soon enough life-calls will echo,
pulling strings of duty taut.
So, sleep, my love, in gentle resting.
Sleep and dreams are dearly bought.

Lullaby

Sleep, my love, and know a resting.
Clear thy brow of hurting things.
Drift upon Love's river lightly
Know a joy that dreaming brings.

Soon enough life-calls will echo,
Pulling strings of duty taut.
So, sleep, my love, in gentle resting;
Sleep and dreams are dearly bought.

MAY TIME

In May
the soft green tips of pine trees reach
into the longer days,
their supplicating fingers
stretch in prayer
toward the ancient sun god's peace.
And brittle laurel branches toughen,
cradling babes
of tight pink blooms,
still in their fetal crouch
beside the new green warrior spikes
of next year's fathering.

In May
the Catbird comes. The Whip-poor-will
falls through the softened air
of moonlit nights to join the sound
of pond-frogs
and the anxious katydids.
Oak leaves unfurl
to send the last brown-leather
wintered shapes to ground
as tenting
for exotic orchid blooms.

In May
the sandy fields awake.
Their wet and rooted darkness yields
a treasure to surpass
the vaults
of neighbor banks
with locks and bars,
and like a beckoning flag delights,
waves strawberries and aspara grass

In May
the school bus, like a ripened pod, expels
the small ones
            on their nature treks, allowed
where just before their bundled forms
had huddled for the schoolroom's warmth
and home again
            to food and hearth—
And promise of June
with long hot days of sun
and silky nights
and wandering minds
to reach—
like supplicating pine trees in the sand.

FOR BROTHER

Once there was a little boy, who
with eyes as blue
as the blue sky where he gazed,
said—"If I were magic—!"
And his baby hands reached
for the wonders that his mind could see.

"But you are not!—
not—
not—
not."
The light went away.
His eyes looked on the ground.

"If I were a Giant—!"
And he stretched himself tall
with tipped toes
and lifted arms
with a great strength.

"But you are not—!
not—
not—
not—
not—
You must see yourself just as you are
and not rely on dreams—"

"If I could fly—!
If I could fly—"

"But you cannot—
cannot—"
"Cannot?
But WHY?"

BALLAD FOR BAD KATE

Oh, Katie was a bad 'un—
the littlest of the lot.
She should've missed the milking
or been sat on at the start.
She should have slept beyond the struggle,
a tiny weary ball,
or chilled beyond a warning
and not heard her mother's call.

Three brothers and five sisters are
a lot of kin to hassle,
when the scales are keyed in ounces
and the big ones win the 'rassle.
Takes a watchful eye to find the speck
a slower puppy misses,
and quick electric jaws to snatch
and get away the fastest—
And when the game is "Let's get Kate,"
to scare the small one sunning—
It takes a sturdy will to stand
and bark instead of running.

Oh Katie was a *bad* 'un!
"Bark" put her first in line,
and soon she learned a show of teeth
need be the only sign.
"Oh, it was just a smile, mom.
See? Didn't mean it mean,
but they are sharp and they are white
so keeps the gaming clean—"

Oh Katie was a bad un,
but not so very bad.
Oh small black dog for loving,
who will not run for fear,
but meets the world's aggression
with dignity and sneer.

BIG GIRL

Black tights kept me neat and warm,
a ribbon pinned a curl.
Bedtime prayers kept the dark away,
but Mama—now I'm a big girl.
I'm bored with playing the princess
protected from nature's cold,
and all those Sabbath day chantings
make me feel stupid and old.
Those things I knew as the trusting child
evoke elementary school.
A whole world spreads across this broad town
and I want to play it all cool.
Don't ask me to love the daughters or boys
of the neighbors that you call friend.
I'm perfectly able to find my own friends
and my home will be open to them!
The roads branch like lace
      from the block where we live.
The hills rise beyond like the sun.
And moonlight draws the tides of me
to the places where life was begun—
I used to believe in all that stuff.
I did—but Mama, I can't.
I'm finding the world and the Sunday school doors
hold a cavern that I resent.
I'm a big girl now, and the voices I hear
don't come from my ancestors' will,
but arrive on the winds of a spinning earth.
And Christ's whisper, I lost in the whirl—

SOUNDINGS

I have come to this place.
There is a message here.
Daily I seek it.
Daily I pray.
But the time has not come—
The message lurks within the shadows
and its soundings stay within the air
until that time my eardrums tighten
and the shadows sort themselves into being.
Daily I listen.
Daily I pray.
But the world is too noisy
and my childhood enfolds me—

MAGIC IS

Magic
is the memory of childhood's wonder—
when all things are new,
and possible—
when love and strength
are but to reach and touch,
and all things touched
are real and beautiful.

Magic
is the memory of feeling real,
of knowing self
as surely as the budded vine
that clings, and seeks to grasp,
yet searches upward,
and sturdy-rooted,
faces toward the sun.

Magic
is the day of memory
when darkness fades with blessed light
and reaching fingers dare
to touch a heaven
and enter
as a little child again.

II
WOMANHOOD

ADAPTATION

There is a place
at the edge of a scream,
where the old years' tangled vines
force new growing.
It hurts
like the promise of breasts
upon the girl-child.
All the ache
and the hurt
and the despair of loss
of what was,
growing into what is
and will be,
becomes a swelling;
becomes a reaching
toward the sun; the light.

There is a place
where the light shines.
But the vines are not dead.
The old dry stems
the jungled growing
suffocates
strangles,
but beyond
is the scream,
and beyond that
is the light no more.
The hurt
the ache
the new greening is better comfort.

TRAIN RIDE, 1942

I took a train to Schenectady,
and little I knew what I would see,
little I knew what the years would bring,
little I knew the songs I'd sing.
But the wheels told a chant as in storybook-ery,
Schenectady—Schen-ect-ady—

October sun on Maple's glow,
October rain before the snow,
October rest at end of year,
Forever afterward held dear.
And the chanting wheels singing to me,
Schenectady—Schenectady—

There it was that the wheels were stilled
and the sighing steam from the boiler filled
the sharp October station air—
The train had stopped, and I was there.
Little I knew what was to be
except what brown eyes promised me.

A hand, a gift, a kiss, a rose,
symbols of heart and mind that knows
the lilting life-tune to share with me
beyond cobbled streets of Schenectady.
I took the hand that was offered to me
and traveled on from Schenectady.

ALL THE ROOMS

I remember all the rooms wherein I slept
and dreamed, and woke again
to clutter of the day before and promise
of a day beginning.
I remember now the colors
of the sunlight
and the places shadows crept.
I swell with fullness of the memories
as one within their likeness
yet a-pulse with change;
each dear and clinging
yet becoming cupped in time.
All the special burdens of decision
have been eased, for good or wrong,
and now the nubby fabric of the years
drapes warmly round me,
and I choose the day's apparel.

What shall I wear today?
And I remember all the rooms
          wherein I chose.

REFRAIN

Lord,
where I may refrain
from inflicting hurt,
let me harbor it,
keeping it within my own hold,
until it is no longer
my enemy,
but a friend
who will stand beside me
in another need.

CHRISTMAS, 1977

I find that love does ask
such a very large part of me
that I wonder what is left
to hang upon the tree
and say—
This is for me—

But perhaps as Christmas dawns
and the Christchild's prayers are heard
His own forgiveness
there will find
my broken star
to piece and mend.
And leave it shining whole to see—
For me—

AT LAKE GEORGE

He cares so much
he has chosen this quiet time
to invite me to the end of the dock
close to the lapping water
and the familiar curves of the mountains
that are softly wrapped
in warm gray mist this morning.
He has drawn up a folding lounge
for me
to be more comfortable than on the
hard steel of the old red chair,
and he fingers his precious workbook
full of the poems of his thoughts.
He casually sets them aside,
as though they are irrelevant
to the conversation, just out of my reach
so that I ask, are they something
I could read?
Well, no they are not ready.
Well, yes I could, but they are
still to be reworked.
Thoughts require so much re-thinking.
What words to use—what might
be better than the words of another
time?

There are interruptions.
The family has so much to say;
to tell; and I have been waiting
so long to listen. My mind
must divide to share, to not
miss these special moments.
He thinks I am not aware
of the fine meaning of his
printed labors, and he is disappointed.
He does not surely know that my mind
has claimed his worded pictures
and he's disappointed that there
were interruptions.
He cares so much, and he is angry.
All this I know.

AT THE CARE INN

I am their daughter,
or their granddaughter—
For the old eyes see only youth
in those who come.
I am their sister
or the friend of their young years.

I am the face
of the love for which they yearn.
I am the one
for whom they waited all the lonely hours.
Oh joy! The precious Now unfolds us,
and the clasp of hands, the kiss,
is not for me
but for some bright memory
I will never know.

It is not I they see,
for I exist
beyond their world, a stranger.
        "Oh God, I love you!
        You are more beautiful every day!
        I do not lie!
        I could, but I would never!
        I thought you'd never come!"
        "I love you too.
        God rest your soul."
I am not beautiful,
but they see it there—
Implant it with the image that they dream,
and my tears
are of the one that they would have me be.

MY MOTHER DIED TODAY

I loved her
and she went away.
Encased in velvet, like a jewel for care,
her essence is the air I breathe

GOING TO HER FUNERAL

October dressed the trees,
and waited for us there.
Hillsides held the memory
of summer green.
The sun gave cooler nurture
to the shortened day.
A bit of blue remained,
and tawny rose,
before the lavender of night
came down.
And drew the light away

LOVE SHE TENDED

Love she tended like a garden flower,
pouring all the richness of the day
in nourishment to growing.

So let it bed her now,
          in tenderest persuasion.
Let it fold her,
like a cloud within its billows
for the gentlest of sleep
and waking.
Let its smile
be Light upon her
as a beacon.
Heal her
Lead her
Friend her in the lonely journey.
Be a peace upon her now.

MOTHER'S DAY

The night's soft mist that lies upon
      the cool of the lake in Spring
curls with the breeze against the lips
      like a kiss at the edge of time,
brings a peace that the promise of morning
            forgot
and the day's brilliant sun didn't see,
and a presence pervades the lonely heart
to persuade it be stilled
          and wait—

DUST

I swept the floor today—
Into the corners, too—
It was long past due!

I found a silver bobbie-pin,
a long white hair,
and all the days my mother's brush
could have flung them there.

A letter slipped behind the bed.
"Dear Tom," it said.
And time when children loved
flew round my head.

A pink doll shoe,
a page-turned book,
a card in dearest script
in its dark nook.
Dust of times-ago
with thoughts deep-plowed,
I gathered in a heap
and harbor now.

AUNT MARY

In the quiet time I think of you.
I remember you in such ordinary ways.
We seldom know the moments
                    Spirit chooses
to place as stories in the
          foundation of our days
          and build an attitude,
but in the quiet times
a shining comes upon a memory,
and stays.

PAST DAFFODILS

The time for daffodils is past.
I looked today and they were gone.
Once a bold and yellow throng,
The sun too hot, they did not last.

THE CHILDREN OF OUR LOVING

God bless the children of our loving
Unto their children's children's child
Show them thy peace in life's rewarding
As they tend the fields you've plowed.

God bless the children of our loving
Unto their children's children's child.
Show them Thy peace in life's rewarding
as they tend the fields you've plowed.

July 1977.

II
FAITHFUL FRIEND AND LOVER

STAY

There is a place he does not wish to go,
and he is wise.
He stays beside the warm hearth fire
that he knows,
& fondles all the dear bright things
around him there—
The leaping flames
betray the solid contours of his world.
The heated embers
radiate—their glow assures.

I tell him of the cold dark room beyond
And beg a candle flame—
He turns to look, and says it is not there.
A wall enfolds—
I say—no—a door.
Stay, he begs, and watch the fire.

HIS FATE

It is his fate.
Day by day its shadow extends
      a little longer
      a little closer
      a little darker.
The message left among the jumbled genes.
Now speaks and voices of his heritage
will not be stilled but whisper
there among the memories
and gather to be louder
and send echoes
where they do not belong
and are not welcome—

Hush! Hush!
Hear only the music.

The time has come
      to smell the air,
      to feel the warmth of day
          upon the skirt
to drowse with pictures
         of faces
     I have known,
to wake with full moonlight
Shining toward my eyes
and drift into the cold sky
and be as distant as the star.

OLLIE'S IMAGINATION

Ollie's imagination took a flare
when he saw a clear blue sky.
He would say, "That's our sky!
Come on. We have to go get our work
and lay it out and do the plans! We
have work to do."

    "I want to get a little airplane
with just two seats, and Mary and I
can fly all over the world (to the safe parts)
and see the world. I'll get
a little helicopter with just two seats—
      That's our sky, Mary!"

WHERE'S MARY?

Mary?
Where's Mary?
I want Mary.
I love you.
I love you so much
If there is anything
       I could do
to make your life happier,
I would do it.
       I don't want to die.
       Not now.
       Sometime maybe,
       not now—
              Oh, my darling,
              sometime is now.
              Sometime has come
              and it is now.
                     I love you and
                     I have to let you go
                     into the Sometime,
                     as we have always known.

BEDSIDE PRAYER

Come, my God, and be with me
light whereby to hear and see.
Send Your spirit to touch, to stay,
to show my heart and hands the way.
Keep clear the wooded path tonight.
Call back the shadows with Your light.
Use now the hands You gave to me
to lift another's burdens free.

It is Your love that rules the day
and shows the night for false decay,
a resting pulse for lesser things
that cannot bear the ache light brings.
Sustain these aching souls who pray
to understand Your loving way,
to cast it on as You would have
upon the current and the wave.

PINE TREES

I will take my burdens to the pine tree
and lay them there upon the yielding branches
    Like the garlands draped for festival
    Like a layering of snow
    Like the gray fog that comes across the water
        and clings against the greenness
        in droplet dews
        on crystal ice
    to mirror all the rainbows
        of the morning

I will trade them for the breathing
        of the pine trees
I will trade them for the aged truths exhaled
    The nurtured air and sun,
    The rooted soil,
    The storms that come across the water
        give life and strength of soul
        to nature's growing
and my burdens are but scattered mist
        upon the years

NOT A SPRING RAIN

The rain was not a spring rain.
It turned last night to snow
that cases every tree and weed
and whites the ground below.
The wind was not a sweet wind.
It smashed the branches down—
the dead ones; the old ones—
And made a rushing sound.
The sun is not a warm sun.
It's farther than the wind,
but it lights the crystal world like love
and lets the blue come in.

IN THIS PLACE

In this place
at this time
I hold your hand.
      There is no greater need,
      no greater deed,
      than that I stand
beside you now.
And know the warmth
of my soul's blend
      with yours
      upon this moment
      and for your peace,
            my friend.

.

TO SAY GOODBYE

I feel like I have come to say goodbye—
To something—
What am I leaving?
Or what is leaving me?
Where is it going—that which had been?
What can I say?
Can I hold it just a little longer?
Or must I simply go away.

A DAY WITH A FRIEND

We need a day with a friend
for the lonely days
to remember.
And when we recover the day
it's June again
in September!

COLD

Cold claims the spirit, numbs,
then creeps across the body's protests
like a stream that seeps
from springs unknown, hid from
the probing rays of everlasting sun.

Cold comes without a wind.
The spirit does not call
for insulating cloak, or heated wall,
until the rigid body hurts, and pain
suffuses all that spirit gained.

What resting must we know, what crying?
What knowing will release the cold?
And willing, let it be discarded
in the ashes of a time untold?
What light
must needs be brought from where
to temper cold to what soul can bear?

NIGHT HOLDS

The night holds such a mystery of sadness
as though in sleep released, a crying
of all the aching souls
within its weighted air.
The mockery of empty peace
      and gentle darkness
swells like pain amid the crowding,
as every hurt and cry for Deity
that ever rose with steams of time
had joined a shifting pulse
      and mournful singing
while conscious joy
      and manifested beauty
slept, like innocence protected
          from the light.

What message comes? What sobbing burden?
What streams of need and protest
          there to join?
Human soul outside the understanding,
it is for God to love and know and bear.

DARK HARBOR

There lurks a shadow I should shun
Yet knowing that, I let it come
and creep within
to harbor there,
a memory.

Some part of me cannot release
the dark companion walking near,
I allow its reaching to enfold
a tired spirit within cold.

The memory
is vague, yet strong,
and binds me in its heavy dream
until the soul accepts a knowing,
and sends me to the light again.

VILLAGE WALK

Walking through the village
like the mist that flows
among the stones,
I see the stones that are a part
of the rough land
of the sea-bottom shelves,
that now lift toward the light,
the caverned layers.
The green velvet
of growing things soften them;
the holes have settled
to their familiar patterns
and oversee the lace of walls
that land-owning generations
have designed.

Here, the walls have clustered
where neighbor upon neighbor
needed shelter,
and raised these to form
stone-roofed barns
and dwellings
and gardened terraces,
never laying two walls
where one would do,
and chimneying the ends
          for family fires.
Paths grew where footsteps found
a way, and barriers became a step.

Castleton, England

WHO I HAVE BECOME

I.

Sometimes I forget
       how to act; where I am;
       who it is I have become.

I go around with a wrinkled face,
       and yet I am the same person
       I have always known
       when there was no mirror,
       when no one's eyes told me
       who I was expected to be.

I am the same person
       who sat upon my Mother's bed
       and sipped milky tea
       poured from a brown earthenware pot,
       and gazed proudly at a newborn
       brother-babe two years younger
       than myself.

I am the same girl-child
       in a yellow dress
       singing "Farmer in the Dell"
       before the kindergarten fireplace,
       holding hands as one link in a circle
       and my eyes on N.C. Wyeth's
       cloud formed giant
       framed upon the wall.

My Mother ties butterfly bows
       on the top of my head

while I recite multiplication tables
in morning ritual, or she
greets me at the door
with blue questioning eyes
to know how I survived
my high-school oratorical contest.
She helps me choose blue velvet
for my wedding dress.
She appears beside my bed
with my own wide-eyed infant
in her arms, fresh-diapered,
and already making sucking sounds.
She lies dying with the sweetness
of a child and I feel older than she
and hold her close,
and then must let her go.
      But I am the same person.
      There was no mirror there.

II.

Lost in time,
      I touch the stone set in the wall.
      Such old stones
      Set there so long ago
      and marked by wind and rains,
      but the same that were lifted fresh-up
      to their place by hands long a part
      of earth itself.
            Where is the cloud-Giant?
            Is there a ribbon in my hair?
            Where is my precious babe?

I look up to see a red-haired man
and the mirror of his kind eyes
tells me that I wear a wrinkled face.
We smile across the distance
and turn upon our ways,
but I know I shall forget again.

Castleton, England

Sometimes I forget
   how to act; where I am;
   who it is I have become.

I go around with a wrinkled face,
   and yet I am the same person
   I have always known
   when there was no mirror;
   when no one's eyes told me
   who I was expected to be.

FLYING

Cloud patterns
like spilled ink
beneath white smoke

Black dreams
more vivid
than the thought that put them there

A LOT TO THINK ABOUT

You gave me a lot to think about the other day.
I came home and took up again my
                                    writing.
My children were delighted.

They thought that they could see
        my sleeping brain awakening—
That the Mother they had known and
                                    loved
        was again creating.

Thank you for the gentle stirring
        of my thoughts, to live again.

ALL THE SUMMER DAISIES

All the summer daisies have grown tired
and allow themselves to droop.
Their soft and eager whiteness turned to
                                    reflect the sun
is browning on the edges as all the rest
                                     have done.
Each oval pedal wants to curl upon itself
and ignore the neighbor ovals that have
                      befriended it since Spring.

All the summer daisies plan to come again.
That program is in the roots they fed.
Sleep overcomes them and their stiffened stems
do not respond to the damp earth's urging,
do not recognize the sun's bright invitation.
But they will move aside as new greenness crowds
in another summer's growing.

THE CURIOUS CLOUDS

From behind the mountains
they rise to greet the sky,
as though to say,
What have you to amuse us
On this fine day?
They blow and dance, according to the currents
sent from the lake that they pass over
and from the warm field. They prod
the forever blue above them
until it sends its color in shadowed tints
to mingle, leaving sun-bright tips that cheer us
                                    and deny that
they could harbor gray rain for later
                          in the day.

A MAN AND A WOMAN WALK

Along the path they happen on.
It is shadowed. They are lonely,
each one's dreams enveloping,
as an isolating shell.
Every step is its own triumph
and the footprints are not gone.
In leafy shadows shift new patterns,
challenge the new days that come.
A patch of sunlight beams
warm upon the path.
It is welcome, yet should it be feared?
Can it be safely passed?
      Can the dreams be recognized
      by each, and both, and so become
      a sweeter story to be told
      in each friendly sharing?
            Gently evening hovers.

SUNSET ROSE

I love the silhouette of trees,
black against the evening sky
with drifting clouds,
dark about the sunset rose.

I love the glimpse of lake beyond
and the scalloped ridge of distant mountains.
It is my days-end painting
to take with me through darkness
and the night.

NOT JUST FOR TEENS

It's not just for teenagers to fall in love.
We did it at 92.
It happens when Bill smiled his lovely smile
and said, Mary—
I've fallen in love with you.

& love when he saw as beautiful
the face that for 92 years
has shared the world and its stresses,
its joys and sadness and tears.

I love that he brought his music,
his stories and poems and songs,
and I'm glad that he brought his warm body
to sit beside me and dream.

What do you think, Bill? I pled.
I think of you. Just you, he said.

CHANGE

There will be a time of other days
when a moment of change is come.
Don't grieve
too much, but remember
how I have loved you
and all you have been that contented me—

A LITTLE REST

Are you all right?
Yes, I just stopped to take a breather.
Are you tired?
I'm tired. I just take a little rest.
      I look at the flowers
      What kind of bird has that song?
How old are you? You're doing so well. You still have all your
own teeth.
      You have such a nice smile.
Thank you. They are mine with a lot of help.
Oh, I am 81. You are doing so well. God has blessed you.
Yes, god has blessed me. I tell him that every day.

MUSIC AGAIN

When Christmas is past I'll remember
the music I heard today.
The lights and candles,
the crystal and bows
will remain an image
      I can almost hold
and my mind will touch
      in a knowing way
And know it was on Christmas Day.

But now in a dream I wonder
the why of evergreen sprays
the lights and tiny glass angels
and songs from my childhood days.
Dinner again and the candle flame,
ribboned boxes name by name.
It can't be Christmas as Christmas was
in spite of bells and Santa Claus!

But when it is past I'll remember
as if a jewel formed through time.
The angel of love will touch me
and the music will sound again.

THE WAVE OF THE DAY

The wave of the day laps gently
and shifts bits of sand at the shore,
designing a lace-like encounter with time
that with the next wave is no more.
Storms of the season had changed the lay
of a land familiar and dear—
Yet the lace that ripples at waters edge
and traces a delicate untamed thread,
holds a beauty with all that is near.

The wave of the day laps gently
And shifts bits of sand at the shore.
Designing a lace-like encounter with time
That with the next wave is no more.
Storms of the season have changed the lay
Of a land familiar and dear—
Yet the lace that ripples at waters' edge
And traces a delicate untamed thread
Holds a beauty with all that is near,

EPILOGUE

For hospice workers, caregivers, and families losing loved ones—

The poetry reading where we hoped to present the first galley of "Wave of the Day" to its author, our mother Mary Elizabeth Winn, was set for the morning of July 5th. The evening of July 4th, with the sound of fireworks in the distance, Mary took her final breath. The collected poems we had wanted to share during her lifetime became instead the substance of a twilight family memorial on a grassy ledge at our brother's home, overlooking the water on Lake Champlain.

The publication of this book of our mother's poems was originally intended as a gift from her children to her. But in the course of our gathering, selecting, transcribing, editing, and assembling the book's creation, the experience grew into an unexpected, much greater gift—one from her to each of us.

Each grief is so personal I can only speak of how important this was to me. When I revisited her poetic perspectives and insights, each visit's mother-daughter exchange jogged family stories and opened portals for memory retrieval. Sometimes while reading aloud, I would hear her with belabored breath join in on certain lines, our two voices speaking as one.

Another unanticipated gift was the almost eerie way the feelings expressed in certain of her poems matched my own. Poems she had written when she had been caring for her mother who had suffered a stroke four decades earlier gave me language and imagery as I cared for mine. There was "no greater need, no greater deed" than simply to be beside her during this passage.

When the hospice chaplain called one day offering to visit, I asked if she would be open to engaging from the vantage point of my mother's poetry. She told me later that the privilege of being present while I recited a few of them, of hearing during the pauses the anecdotes evoked, the memories triggered, of being part of the short conversations that ensued, were some of the most profound moments of her time as chaplain.

Not everyone will be drawn to this way of sharing at such a critical time. I understand that not everyone's parent writes or paints, or has a particular avenue for creative expression, and that not everyone's parent lives well into their 90's with cognitive function intact. I understand too that we each approach the imminent death of a loved one differently, grieving differently, as evidenced in our own family.

But for those who might find helpful what my ailing mother and I stumbled upon together, here's what my mama taught me in her final few weeks

    —the value of documenting your loved one's life in some way, whether it's with photos, artwork, gardening, songs, knitting, painting, collaging, collecting, letter writing, whether done for love or as a profession.

    —the value of using the palpable legacy of these loves produced over a lifetime to spark and feed memories and communication between you and your parent or loved one, a connection that prompts conversations deeper than does the tired litany of "How are you? Did you sleep all right? How's your pain level? Have you been drinking enough liquids?"

—the value of acknowledging the arts, their power to heal and to connect, not just through what we may typically think of as the arts, such as poetry, painting and music, but the art of things like child-raising, bread-baking, sewing, teaching, gardening. The list of human endeavors and devotions is endless.

—the value of bearing witness on a regular basis to a dying loved one or parent's still operative curiosity, love of learning, ability to give, to learn, to question, to educate, to pass on what they alone or you together might uncover.

This body of work, its process and attentive collaboration, proved to be so helpful to our family in prompting deeper conversations, closeness, and connection, my personal hope is that it can also be of help to others, as well as a valuable resource to hospice workers and caregivers.

—Diana Winn Levine

ABOUT THE AUTHOR

Mary Elizabeth Winn (née Hedgcock), born in Illinois and raised in the upper peninsula of Michigan, was an artist and poet all her life. Wife, mother, pilot, painter, sculptor, doll maker, author, and college graduate of Skidmore College at the age of 83—through all of it, she was writing poems. Mary lived her last years in Shelburne, Vermont near her children. She was born on Christmas Eve 1921 and died on the 4th of July 2016.

Her previous book of poetry and watercolors for children is entitled *Pictures of the Pinelands,* and is available from Rootstock Publishing, www.rootstockpublishing.com.